INVOCA

INVOCATIONS TO LAKSHMI

Ashima Singh

Series Editor: Shalini Saran

VIKING

VIKING

Penguin Books India (P) Ltd., 11 Community Centre, Panchsheel Park, New Delhi 110 017, India
Penguin Books Ltd., 80 Strand, London WC2R 0RL, UK
Penguin Putnam Inc., 375 Hudson Street, New York, NY 10014, USA
Penguin Books Australia Ltd., 250 Camberwell Road, Camberwell, Victoria 3124, Australia
Penguin Books Canada Ltd., 10 Alcorn Avenue, Suite 300, Toronto, Ontario, M4V 3B2, Canada
Penguin Books (NZ) Ltd., Cnr Rosedale and Airborne Roads, Albany, Auckland, New Zealand

First published in Viking by Penguin Books India 2002

Copyright © Ashima Singh 2002

All rights reserved

10 9 8 7 6 5 4 3 2 1

Typeset in AGaramond by S.R. Enterprises
Printed at Saurabh Print-O-Pack, Noida

This book is sold subject to the condition that it shall not, by way of trade or otherwise, be lent, resold, hired out, or otherwise circulated without the publisher's prior written consent in any form of binding or cover other than that in which it is published and without a similar condition including this condition being imposed on the subsequent purchaser and without limiting the rights under copyright reserved above, no part of this publication may be reproduced, stored in or introduced into a retrieval system, or transmitted in any form or by any means (electronic, mechanical, photocopying, recording or otherwise), without the prior written permission of both the copyright owner and the above-mentioned publisher of this book.

ॐ श्रीं श्रिये नमः।

Aum Shreem Shriyey Namah

I pay obeisance to the glory of the Exalted One.

AUTHOR'S NOTE

Spiritual growth is independent of religious beliefs. Religion and rituals can serve as guides and they can help discipline the seeker, but the actual process of spiritual growth is totally non-religious. The inner self needs to be in tune with the Absolute Divine Self for optimum utilization of the inner forces. Spiritual growth is related to the refining of cognitive perceptions of the entire range of emotions, expectations, desires and experiences which then makes us aware enough to realize that we are manifestations of the same Absolute Source of all creation.

INTRODUCTION

Unlike with other goddesses, there is only one great myth associated with Lakshmi: the myth of the *Samudra Manthan* or the 'Churning of the Ocean of Milk'.

When Indra, the king of the gods, lost everything to the demons due to the disrespect shown to the great, but ill-tempered sage Durvasa, he was advised by Lord Vishnu to reconcile with his enemies, the demons, with whose help the ocean of milk would have to be churned. The churning would produce *amrit* or ambrosia. On drinking this nectar, the gods would become immortal and regain all that they had lost.

So the gods and the demons made Mount Mandara the churning rod. Vishnu took the form of Kurma, a gigantic tortoise, to support the mountain on his back. The great serpent Vasuki was used as the churning rope.

4

The first product to emerge from the churning was Halaahal, the most deadly poison. Shiva swallowed this poison on everybody's request, for as Mahadev, he was the only one capable of countering its ill effects. Then emerged Kamdhenu, the wish-fulfilling cow; Ucchaishrav, the white horse; Airavata, the elephant; Kaustubhmani, the matchless jewel; Kalpavriksha, the wish-fulfilling tree; Apsaras, the celestial nymphs; Alakshmi or Jyeshtha, the counterpoint of Lakshmi; Lakshmi the goddess of abundance and good fortune; Varuni, the goddess of wine; Dhanvantri, the physician of the gods, bearing the pot of amrit in his hands and finally, the conch.

The sages took the cow; Vishnu took the conch and the Kaustubhmani; Indra took the elephant and the wish-fulfilling tree and the king of demons took the horse.

Lakshmi expressed her wish to marry the perfect male, unblemished by flaws and weaknesses. Thus, she chose to dwell in Vishnu's heart as he was the immortal who possessed the finest qualities and whose character was untainted; the one who represented perfection in all aspects.

* * * * *

Shree or Lakshmi embodies grace and beauty and is the goddess of abundance, good fortune and prosperity. The Mother Goddess as a symbol of fertility, water and agriculture is common to all ancient civilizations. It is believed that Shree was this pre-Vedic Mother Goddess who was later merged into the goddess Lakshmi. Lakshmi is the Universal Mother—Lokmata and Jaganmata— the benevolent nourisher of the entire universe. She presides over the fertility and moisture of the soil and over the jewels and precious metals in the womb of the earth, and is depicted as sitting or standing on a lotus, which is the universal womb.

Normally associated with material wealth, Lakshmi is, in fact, the goddess of good fortune and abundance at all levels—body, mind and consciousness, for she also bestows that wisdom which leads to eternal bliss. She is also the symbolic representation of any achievement, the ultimate reward for every endeavour.

As Bhuvaneshwari, the goddess of the cosmos, Lakshmi increases verdure, helps the girl child grow into a procreating entity, urges the sperm to fertilize the egg, the seed to grow into a tree and the flower, to fruit. She is, thus, that energy which oversees the welfare and prosperity of all creatures on earth.

Lakshmi is also the energy which leads us to an awareness of the origin and purpose of our birth and permeates us with the rich and beautiful realization that we can be what we invoke. She keeps us in comfort, protects us from deprivation, helps us to enjoy the best of everything life has to offer and also bestows on us the wisdom that helps us to appreciate the miracle of life.

The consort of Vishnu, the Preserver, she is the vibrant, female energy which activates the male energy of Vishnu. Lakshmi nourishes, Vishnu preserves.

Vishnu the Father, provides; Lakshmi the Mother, nurtures. Narayan or Vishnu, is the Divine Supreme Being; Lakshmi is Narayani, the Mother. We are children of the Divine. It is their combined energies which can lead us to the profound realization, 'I Am That' or *So Hum*.

*****

According to the *Puranas*, Lakshmi in her first incarnation was the daughter of the sage Brighu and his wife Khyati.

However, as the consort of Vishnu, she was also born as his spouse in his various incarnations. Thus, when Vishnu was born as Vaaman, the dwarf son of Aditi, Lakshmi appeared from the lotus as Padma or Kamala. When he was born as Parasurama, she was Dharani; when he was Ramachandra, she was Sita and when he was Krishna, she was Rukhmini. Thus if Vishnu took a celestial form, she appeared as divine; if Vishnu became a mortal she too would take a mortal form, transforming her own person to fit whatever character Vishnu assumed.

8

In his supreme state, Vishnu is one with his consort who represents his power and energy. The *Vishnu Purana* says 'Sri, the bride of Vishnu, the Mother of the world, is eternal, imperishable; as he is all-pervading, so she is omnipresent. Vishnu is meaning, she is speech; Hari is polity, she is prudence; Vishnu is understanding, she is intellect; he is righteousness, she is devotion; Sri is earth, Hari is its support. In a world of gods, animals and man, Hari is all that is called male; Lakshmi is all that is termed female; for there is nothing else than they.'

Vishnu is the cosmic water itself, the infinite ocean of that liquid life substance out of which all the various elements of the universe arise, and back into which they must dissolve. Thus Lakshmi, the lotus goddess, is the appropriate consort of Vishnu, for the lotus, through its appearance, gives proof of the life-supporting power of the all-nourishing abyss. This radiant lotus of the world is the goddess Padma, the *shakti* or divine energy of the slumbering Vishnu.

As the consort of Vishnu there are two popular images of Lakshmi. When the world is at peace Vishnu rests on the thousand-hooded serpent, Anant, or Sheshnag, symbolizing the universal living waters. The serpent supports the human form of the divine sleeper, Vishnu. Lakshmi is portrayed as sitting at Vishnu's feet. The other popular image depicts Lakshmi in her supreme aspect—sitting alongside Vishnu on Garuda, the mythical bird.

Garuda is a symbol of the most exalted bird. When on Garuda, Vishnu and Lakshmi symbolize energy which bestows upon us richness and the ability to enjoy the benefits of both the physical and spiritual worlds. It is the energy of the benevolent protector who seeks to restore order.

Garuda clutches a snake in his claws. The snake, which has been tamed by the huge bird, symbolizes lust and a lower existence. In contrast, Garuda, soaring above in the sky denotes the unbound spirit which roams as freely as a bird and is disentangled from the fetters of the earth. He represents the higher, spiritual principle which has been released from the bondage of matter.

Just as this huge bird flies high, similarly our thoughts can make us aware of that which is beyond the bodily senses. It truly means that one has to be able to understand the purpose and meaning of existing in the physical, emotional and spiritual realms—transcending the first two to eventually enjoy the wisdom of the ultimate truth. For when feelings and emotions are purified they translate into pure wisdom.

Lakshmi is also depicted as riding an owl. Here, she represents wealth which has been acquired secretly or unlawfully, for the owl can only see at night and is blinded by daylight. Such wealth may give material comfort but it can give neither peace of mind nor inner prosperity, neither the feeling of richness nor the joy of opulence. Invariably, the one who has acquired wealth in this manner will suffer bad health. The person's nature becomes conspiratorial and is abound with negative emotions. These negative emotions eventually reside in the person, manifesting themselves as chronic physical ailments.

Lakshmi is usually worshipped with Ganesha on the night of Diwali. She had stated that wherever Ganesha is worshipped, she too will reside there.

Our physical body receives a lot of nourishment from the sun, air and earth through the seven basic energy centres located in our auric or etheric body. These energy centres are called *chakras* because they are seen as whorls of energy. When these chakras rotate clockwise they draw energy from the elements to nourish the physical body. Any impurity accrued in our physical or mental field of energy is seen as being dispelled from the body when the chakra moves anticlockwise.

The root chakra draws energy from the earth and represents our basic existence. It is ruled by Ganesha. This chakra is vital for good health and the continuous division and multiplication of our cells. When invoked, Ganesha and Lakshmi together bring material wealth, and people attain physical joy, comfort as well as worldly possessions.

* * * * *

Lakshmi is known by many names: Haripriya, the beloved of Hari (Vishnu); Padma, the lotus; Padmalayaa, she who dwells on a lotus; Jaladhijaa, ocean-born; Chanchala, the fickle one; Dharani, the earth; Shree, the goddess of prosperity and glory; Bhudevi, the goddess of agricultural prosperity and Ramaa, the all-pervasive one. And all these aspects and qualities are reflected in her iconography.

The iconography of Lakshmi reveals the many aspects of the energy she represents. When she is depicted as the consort of Vishnu, the dark one, her complexion is dark. If Lakshmi's complexion is golden yellow, it symbolizes her as the source of all wealth; if white, it is symbolic of her being the purest form of *prakriti* or nature, from which the whole universe emerged. Lakshmi is, however, most commonly depicted as having a pink complexion like the lotus. This symbolizes her compassion for all creatures since she is the Universal Mother.

Her green blouse represents fecundity, verdure and the richness of nature. She is usually depicted as standing or seated on a lotus, bearing a lotus in each of her two hands. She is adorned with a garland of lotuses and is flanked by bejewelled elephants sprinkling her with water drawn from golden pots.

Lakshmi seated on a lotus represents wealth—whether material or spiritual—in every form and at every level. As a symbol, the lotus is integral to Lakshmi.

The lotus thrives in stagnant, murky waters but blossoms with perfection. It is the first sign of perfect life upon the vastness of the primordial waters. It is also a universal, sacred symbol. The Chinese looked upon the pink lotus as a symbol of love; the Hindus saw it as a symbol of prosperity. For the Greeks the pink lotus represented indolent happiness; in the Buddhist mantra

Aum Mani Padme Hum, the light of the essence of being is likened to the jewel in the lotus.

The crown of saints is always depicted as a fully blossomed thousand-petalled lotus, which represents divine knowledge. Thus, the Hindus see the thousand-petalled lotus as a symbol of spiritual fulfilment. The more rare blue lotus is a symbol of Shiva. The Chinese revered the blue lotus as a symbol of royalty.

When Lakshmi stands beside Vishnu, she is shown with two hands. When alone, she is depicted as having four hands and is seated or standing on a lotus throne. She holds a lotus, a conch, a pot of ambrosia and a *bilva* (woodapple) or a pomegranate fruit. These four hands also symbolize the power to grant the four aspects of human existence—*dharma* or righteousness, *artha* or wealth, *kaama* or the pursuit of desire and *moksha* or salvation.

The lotus she bears represents pure thought emerging from the chaos of life. The conch symbolizes water, from which life emerged, and the pot of ambrosia is symbolic of the bliss of immortality. While the bilva fruit represents direct knowledge and moksha the pomegranate signifies worldly possessions. When Lakshmi is depicted with eight hands, holding a bow and arrow, and a mace and discus as well, she represents Mahalakshmi, an aspect of Durga.

★ ★ ★ ★ ★

King Bhoja of Ujjain used to worship the Ashta Lakshmis every day, and thus enjoyed their blessings. One day they appeared before him looking unhappy. The king questioned their unhappiness. They replied that while they were happy with his worship they would have to leave him. However, they said that they would grant him a boon before they departed. The next day, seven of the eight Lakshmis took their leave from him. The last one to leave was Dhairya Lakshmi. The king exercised his boon and prayed to her not to abandon him. Thus, Dhairya Lakshmi remained. The next morning, the king found that the other Lakshmis had returned. They said that wherever Dhairya Lakshmi stayed, the other Lakshmis would reside there too.

The following are the eight forms or aspects of the energy which Lakshmi symbolizes.

As Adyalakshmi, she is the primordial source of wealth, derived from the elements. The *panchabhuta*, the five elements of air, earth, water, fire and ether or *aakaash*, are primeval, eternal wealth. Man's existence depends upon these as does the existence of all living beings. As Adyalakshmi, the goddess awakens the ability to feel rich. Along with the possession of riches it is also necessary for us to have the joy within to appreciate it all. All types of wealth and accolades are meaningless unless we have the ability to enjoy them.

Vidyalakshmi is the dispeller of ignorance. She bestows on us an abundance of knowledge, which gives us the wisdom and the skill to decide upon our goals. Only through knowledge can we achieve these goals.

Dhanalakshmi bestows prosperity and opulence. They are seen to be of eight different kinds: *aishwarya* or grandeur; gold and the nine jewels; power and position;

progeny; food; transportation; emotional sustenance and lastly, manpower.

Kaamalakshmi is symbolic of *rajas*, the power which motivates and creates the desire to acheive and acquire.

Just as Kaamalakshmi creates and fulfils desires, similarly Vijayalakshmi symbolizes the desire to triumph.

Satyalakshmi represents truth. She is the one who reveals the essence and reality of the ultimate truth.

Bhogalakshmi is invoked to bless us with the ability to appreciate and enjoy the riches of this world.

All the various aspects of the energy which Lakshmi symbolizes converge in Yogalakshmi. Yogalakshmi is also known as Dhairyalakshmi. Dhairya means patience and it is patience which allows the confluence of these energies. Yogalakshmi is invoked to secure all finer energies to prevent their dissipation.

Alakshmi is the counterpoint of Lakshmi. Alakshmi is poverty; she is the personification of misfortune. She too emerged when the ocean of milk was churned. Since she appeared first she is also known as Jyeshtha or the elder one. She is visualized as an old woman with a broom in her hand, riding an ass. A crow adorns her banner.

* * * * *

We are usually preoccupied with our needs, desires and destinies. Most people stop at the belief that destiny is not meant to be tampered with. However, once we have the wisdom to improve our skills and abilities, we can change our situation through sheer discipline and motivated action. It is often heard that only the lucky ones are rewarded for their efforts. Luck is the combination of everything that one puts into the end in focus. Effort is useless without faith in the result, faith in our achievement. *Shraddaavan labhatey gyaanam* signifies that faith directs us towards that wisdom which will help us achieve our goals.

Our five senses are linked to the five elements: touch to air; taste to water; smell to earth; sight to fire, the light of the sun and hearing to space which is represented by ether, the all-pervading, radiant energy that fills the universe. When space is energized through sound, the first four senses of touch, taste, smell and sight work in tandem and a complete mobilization of faculties takes place. Therein lies the value of an invocation.

A true invocation, unlike a ritual one, requires an awareness of our priorities, which enables us to decide whom or which energy to invoke. It is offered in the belief that it will bear a response. Our own energies have to work with spatial energy through sound to achieve our goal. When a karate expert breaks a brick into two halves with one precise movement of the hand, it is not the contact between the hand and the brick alone that is of importance. The expert is also addressing the space between the hand and the brick. This is an amalgamation of the power of thought, and the speed with which it was sent to the object.

The invocation offered aloud, is also preceded by certain actions which help in the process of purifying and focusing our thoughts. It is, however, important not to get trapped in the actions, symbols or rituals alone but to use these as a means of reaching the essence of the final energy.

Lakshmi as an energy is invoked for longevity, prosperity, good health, healthy progeny and wealth and opulence at all levels.

Before invoking the Supreme Source of all blessings and bounties, we must prepare our physical and mental body to be receptive to these blessings. Every cell in the body has an electrical charge, like everything around us. The electrical charge is a form of energy and is influenced by our way of life. Sometimes the level of energy is low and our motor system works slowly; sometimes energy flies through us and we feel we can take on the world.

Energy meridians run vertically and more or less parallel, from head to toe. The living organism can be influenced at different points along these energy meridians. There are fourteen energy points along these meridians.

The ritual for making the physical body and meridians more receptive involves the touching of the various points to activate the receptors. However, what you receive in return is a matter of faith as well as karmic entitlement.

Touch the sternum or the centre of your chest, forehead, the top of your head, and your shoulders with your hands crossed. Then touch your right and left eyes and ears and finally the base of your spine and your ankles. Then move your right hand clockwise around your head, snap your fingers and clap your hands.

These actions activate the heart and forehead, and protect the *antahkarna* or spiritual cord at the top of the head which is like an antennae for receiving divine blessings. Touching the shoulders with crossed arms connects the two sides of the body, the yin and yang. Moving the right hand over the head is that action which wishes away any interfering energy, any negative force entering your space while you are invoking the goddess.

To invoke Lakshmi, we must first invoke and invite Ganesha. As lord of our cellular structure Ganesha is symbolic of prayers offered with the entirety of our being. He clears the way for the devotee. His blessings are required first to enable us to absorb the benevolence of Lakshmi and the bounty bestowed upon us by her. Either the mantra *Aum Shree Ganeshaaya Namah* or the one that follows may be chanted.

वक्रतुंड महाकाय सूर्यकोटिसमप्रभ।
निर्विघ्नं कुरु मे देव सर्वकार्येषु सर्वदा।।

Vakratunda mahaakaaya sooryakotisamaprabha
Nirvighnam kuru mey deva sarvakaaryeshu sarvadaa.

You of the curved trunk and massive body with the brilliance and light of a million suns, bless my endeavours and remove all obstacles that may hinder my path. Bless me forever.

Then, get an image of Lakshmi or visualize Lakshmi in your mind. Specify your name, location, the date, day and time. By doing this, you are making a commitment, forming a resolution: 'I am sitting here to invoke the blessings of Lakshmi.' The seat should be red in colour and preferably of woollen material.

Facing west, say: 'O great goddess Lakshmi, I invoke you for your blessings.' Keep a pot of water and a lighted lamp in front of her.

After invoking Lakshmi thus, offer her a place, a corner or a shrine as well as something to sit upon, such as an ornate cloth. Then sprinkle some water on her. Make an offering of the *panchamrit*—milk, yogurt, clarified butter, honey and Ganga water—for her to bathe. Present her with clothes, sandalwood paste, vermilion and flowers. Light incense for fragrance, a candle or lamp as well as camphor. Finally, offer her fruit and money. After thanking her, call out the name of Vishnu three times:

Aum Vishnavey Namah
Aum Vishnavey Namah
Aum Vishnavey Namah

THE MAHAALAKSHMI
ASHTAKAM STOTRAM

According to mythology, Indra, the king of the gods, sang the Mahaalakshmi Ashtakam Stotram, a hymn of eight verses in praise of Lakshmi when the goddess emerged on a lotus from the ocean of milk. Lakshmi was so pleased when she heard it, that she said she would forever bless the devotee who sang this hymn.

इन्द्र उवाचः

नमस्तेऽस्तु महामाये श्री पीठे सुरपूजिते।
शंखचक्रगदाहस्ते महालक्ष्मि नमोऽस्तु ते।।

Indra Uvaach:
Namastestu Mahaamaayey shree peethey surapoojitey
Shankhachakragadaahastey Mahaalakshmi namostu tey.

As Indra, the king of the gods, said:

I invoke you, grand goddess, seated on an exalted throne, bearing in your hands a conch, a whirring discus and a mace, and worshipped by the gods, Mahaalakshmi, I pay obeisance to you.*

---

* *The conch represents water; the whirring discus or chakra represents time; the mace symbolizes a mass of concentrated energy.*

नमस्ते गरुडारूढे कोलासुरभयङ्करि।
सर्वपापहरे देवि महालक्ष्मि नमोऽस्तु ते।।

Namaste Garudaaroodhey Kolaasurabhayankari
Sarvapaapharey devi, Mahaalakshmi namostu tey.

My salutations to you who rides Garuda and strikes terror in the demon Kol.* Absolver of all sins, Mahaalakshmi I bow to you.

---

* Garuda is the mythical bird and Vishnu's mount. Lakshmi in her supreme form is seated beside Vishnu on Garuda. The bird is symbolic of space and the soaring spirit. Kolaasura, the demon Kol, is symbolic of the fears which reside within us.

सर्वज्ञे सर्ववरदे सर्वदुष्टभयङ्करि।
सर्वदुखहरे देवि महालक्ष्मि नमोऽस्तु ते।।

Sarvagyey sarvavaradey sarvadushtabhayankari
Sarvadukhaharey devi, Mahaalakshmi namostu
   tey.

Omniscient one, bestower of all blessings, who annihilates all negative forces; the vanquisher of all sorrows, Mahaalakshmi I bow to you.*

---

* *The negative forces which are annihilated are lust, greed, anger, jealousy, egotism, hatred and arrogance.*

सिद्धिबुद्धिप्रदे देवि भुक्तिमुक्तिप्रदायिनि।
मन्त्रमूर्ते सदा देवि महालक्ष्मि नमोऽस्तु ते।।

*Siddhibuddhipradey devi bhuktimuktipradaayini
Mantramoortey sadaa devi, Mahaalakshmi namostu
tey.*

O goddess who bestows upon us the ability to achieve perfection and attain wisdom, who enables us to enjoy the best this world has to offer and liberates us from hankering after desire, who is invoked and energized by the chanting of this mantra, Mahaalakshmi I bow to you.

आद्यान्त रहिते देवि आद्यशक्ति महेश्वरि।
योगजे योग सम्भूते महालक्ष्मि नमोऽस्तु ते।।

Aadhyaanta rahitey devi, aadhyashakti maheshvari
Yogajey yoga sambhootey, Mahaalakshmi namostu tey.

O goddess without beginning or end, primal energy, grand goddess, you who have assimilated all the energies into your being, who are above the spell of illusion and are manifest only through concentrated devotion, Mahaalakshmi I bow to you.

स्थूलसूक्ष्म महारौद्रै महाशक्ति महोदरे।
महापापहरे देवि महालक्ष्मि नमोऽस्तु ते।।

*Sthoolasookshma mahaaraudraiy mahaashakti
    mahodarey
Mahaapaapaharey devi, Mahaalakshmi namostu
    tey.*

Primal causal energy, who has conquered the gross and the subtle; the all-powerful womb of creation, who can annihilate the severest of afflictions, Mahaalakshmi I bow to you.

पद्मासनस्थिते देवि परब्रह्मस्वरूपिणि।
परमेशि जगन्मातर्महालक्ष्मि नमोऽस्तु ते।।

Padmaasanasthitey devi parabrahmasvaroopini
Parameshi jaganmaatarmahaalakshmi namostu tey.

O goddess seated on a lotus, manifest form of the Supreme Being, O supreme goddess who governs the laws of nature, Mahaalakshmi I bow to you.*

---

* *The lotus is the seat of wisdom and knowledge. It is the symbol of purity for it rises in its beauty, above murky waters. At a simpler level, it also represents the plant kingdom which Lakshmi nurtures.*

श्वेताम्बरधरे देवि नानालङ्कारभूषिते।
जगत्स्थिते जगन्मातर्महालक्ष्मि नमोऽस्तु ते।।

*Shvetaambaradharey devi
    naanaalankaarabhooshitey
Jagatsthitey jaganmaatarmahaalakshmi namostu
    tey.*

The following three shlokas are usually recited after the Mahaalakshmi Ashtakam Stotram.

O goddess dressed in white and adorned with many jewels, you energize all of nature by your presence and all realms come into being by your grace. Sustainer of the world, Mahaalakshmi I bow to you.*

---

* *White symbolizes* sattva, *the essence of pure energy. The many jewels which adorn Lakshmi are symbolic of the colours of nature. All the colours are contained in the colour white.*

महालक्ष्म्यष्टकं स्तोत्रं यः पठेद्भक्तिमान्नरः।
सर्वसिद्धिमवाप्नोति राज्यं प्राप्नोति सर्वदा।।

*Mahaalakshmyashtakam stotram yah pathedbhaktimaannarah
Sarvasiddhimavaapnoti raajyam praapnoti sarvadaa.*

He who reads this Mahaalakshmyashtakam with devotion and concentration becomes worthy of attaining all perfections and becomes the master of his own self.

एक काले पठेनित्यं महापापविनाशनम्।
द्विकालं य: पठेनित्यं धनधान्य समन्वित:।।

*Eka kaaley pathenityam
  mahaapaapavinaashanam
Dvikaalam yah pathenityam dhanadhaanya
  samanvitah.*

He who reads it once daily is absolved of his gravest sins. He who reads it twice daily will receive every manner of wealth and riches.

त्रिकालं य: पठेनित्यं महाशत्रुविनाशनम्।
महालक्ष्मीभवेनित्यं प्रसन्ना वरदा शुभा।।

Trikaalam yah pathenityam
 mahaashatruvinaashanam
Mahaalakshmeebhavenityam prasannaa
 varadaa shubhaa.

He who reads it three times daily has his most powerful enemies vanquished, and will remain the favourite of the auspicious Mahaalakshmi who bestows her blessings forever.*

---

* *The powerful enemies are within us. They are the fearful emotions of greed, lust, anger, jealousy and hatred. Overcoming these purifies and liberates a person.*

THE SHREE SOOKTAM

The Shree Sooktam, which literally means verses to the goddess Shree, belongs to the latter part of the *Rig Veda*. It is considered to be the ultimate invocation to Shree or Lakshmi.

The invocation is made through Agni, the god of fire. It was common practice in Vedic times, as defined in the *Rig Veda*, to offer prayers through a fire sacrifice (*havan* or *yagna*) because fire and heat signified life. The flame is seen as part of the great Divine Light. Thus, when prayers along with oblations are offered to the fire, they are symbolically being offered to the highest form of the Divine Light.

Agni is invoked as the carrier of energy. By praying to Agni, the prayer is carried to the source of all creation. Therefore all offerings in the havan are made to Agni who acts as a witness to every sacred ritual.

Before reciting the Shree Sooktam the devotee should sit facing the north or east, the two centres of positive energy, and meditate on Lakshmi, seated on a lotus, holding a lotus in one hand, while from the other hand golden light emanates in the *varamudra*, the gesture denoting blessing.

Then the devotee should light a lamp and say:

'Here I sit beside this light, symbolic of the bigger source of light and energy, asking for the well-being of my family. I ask for the boon of prosperity and the fulfilment of all my desires at all levels of existence. I pray to the divine benevolent Lakshmi to make my home her abode and shower the blessings of fulfilment forever. So I am reciting the Shree Sooktam.'

In Vedic times women and lower caste people were forbidden to recite the Shree Sooktam for fear of mispronunciation. The post-Vedic period saw the Shree Sooktam replaced by the Lakshmi Sookta, written in a simpler language so that it could by recited easily by everyone.

Dhyaan Mantra

This Dhyaan Mantra is chanted before reciting the Shree Sooktam.

Dhyaan Mantra

या सा पद्मासनस्था विपुलकटितटी पद्मपत्रायताक्षी
गम्भीरावर्तनाभिस्तनभरनमिता शुभ्रवस्त्रोत्तरीया।
लक्ष्मीदिव्यैर्गजेन्द्रैर्मणिगणरखचितैः स्नापिता हेमकुम्भै-
र्नित्यं सा पद्महस्ता मम गृहे वसतु सर्वमांगल्ययुक्ता।।

*Yaa saa padmaasanasthaa vipulakatitatee
    padmapatraayataakshee
Gambheeraavartanaabhistanabharanmitaa
    shubhravastrottareeyaa.
Lakshmeedivyaiyrganjendrairmaniganakhachitaih
    snaapitaa hemakumbhaiy
Nityam saa padmahastaa mama grihey vasatu
    sarvamaangalyayukttaa.*

May that Lakshmi born of a lotus and seated on a lotus, with a deep and round navel, and eyes like the petals of a lotus, bent with the fullness of her breasts, wearing bright garments, bathed with water drawn from golden, bejewelled pots by celestial elephants, with a lotus in her hand, ever dwell in my house with all her auspicious qualities.

ॐ हिरण्यवर्णां हरिणीं सुवर्णरजतस्रजाम्।
चन्द्रां हिरण्मयीं लक्ष्मीं जातवेदो म आ वह।।

*Aum hiranyavarnaam harineem
   suvarnarajatasrajaam
Chandraam hiranmayeem Lakshmeem jaatavedo
   ma aa vaha.*

O Agni, god of fire, since you are witness to the past, present and future, I implore you to please invoke Mahaalakshmi for me. Please help me to invoke the golden-coloured great goddess Lakshmi, who nurtures the plant kingdom and all life forms, who wears gold and silver ornaments and garlands of white flowers and who is radiant with the light of knowledge. May her radiance shine upon me like the soothing light of the moon. Please invite Lakshmi for me.*

---

* *Lakshmi's gold and silver ornaments represent the energy of the sun and the moon.*

तां म आ वह जातवेदो लक्ष्मीमनपगामिनीम्।
यस्यां हिरण्यं विन्देयं गामश्वं पुरुषानहम्।।

*Taam ma aa vaha jaatavedo
   Lakshmeemanapagaamineem
Yasyaam hiranyam vindeyam gaamashvam
   purushaanaham.*

O god of fire, please invoke Lakshmi for me with your energies. As jewels and metals reside within the earth, so, too, may Lakshmi reside within my house and never desert me. I seek her grace, abundance, sustenance and all the worldly comforts. I wish to be endowed with the blessings of the Divine Mother.

अश्वपूर्वां रथमध्यां हस्तिनादप्रमोदिनीम्।
श्रियं देवीमुप ह्वये श्रीर्मा देवी जुषताम्।।

*Ashvapoorvaam rathamadhyaam
    hastinaadapramodineem
Shriyam deveemupa hvayey shreermaa devi
    jushataam.*

Goddess Shree, sustainer of all life forms, who comes in a chariot drawn by white horses, whose arrival is heralded by the trumpeting of elephants, I invoke that goddess to please bless me by staying permanently in my abode.

कां सोस्मितां हिरण्यप्राकारामार्द्रीं ज्वलन्तीं तृप्तां तर्पयन्तीम्।
पद्मे स्थितां पद्मवर्णाम् तामिहोप ह्वये श्रियम्।।

*Kaam sosmitaam hiranyapraakaaraamaadraam
  jvalanteem triptaam tarpayanteem
Padmey sthitaam padmavarnaam taamihopa
  hvayey shriyam.*

She is lustrous and ever-smiling and she dwells in radiance in her compassion, she fulfils desires like moisture impregnates the thirsting earth. Her glory is inexplicable and immeasurable. Brimming with joy she fills everyone with unbounded happiness. She is seated on a lotus and is the embodiment of compassion.

चन्द्रां प्रभासां यशसा ज्वल्न्तीं श्रियं लोके देवजुष्टामुदाराम्।
तां पद्मिनीमीं शरणं प्रपद्ये ऽअलक्ष्मीर्मे नश्यतां त्वां वृणे।।

*Chandraam prabhaasaam yashasaa jvalanteem
   shriyam lokey devajushtaamudaaraam
Taam padmineemeem sharanam prapadhyey
   Alakshmeermey nashyataam tvaam vriney.*

She shines in her own glory, like the moon, and is worshipped joyfully by gods and humans alike. She is extremely generous to those who worship her. I seek refuge in her glory and compassion. O goddess, please vanquish my inner poverty with your blessings.

आदित्यवर्णे तपसोऽधि जातो वनस्पतिस्तव वृक्षो ऽथ बिल्वः।
तस्य फलानि तपसा नुदन्तु या अन्तरा याश्च बाह्या
अलक्ष्मीः।।

Aadityavarney tapasoadhi jaato vanaspatistava vriksho ath bilvah
Tasya falaani tapasaa nudantu yaa antaraa yaashcha baahya Alakshmeeh.

Your exalted radiance is like that of the sun. You are the source of energy, like the sun. O benevolent one, insufficient knowledge causes ignorance. O goddess of the plant kingdom, from your glow the bilva fruit appeared directly, without flowering. I offer the same fruit to you to seek your blessings for direct knowledge.*

---

* *Alakshmi is symbolic of poverty. The divine fruit, bilva, is born of the king of trees which fruits without flowering. The bilva therefore symbolizes direct knowledge. Lakshmi symbolizes true riches. If you don't feel fulfilled within, you cannot be called rich.*

उपैतु मां देवसख: कीर्तिश्च मणिना सह।
प्रादुर्भूतोऽस्मि राष्ट्रेऽस्मिन्कीर्तिमृद्धिं ददातु मे।।

Upaitu maam devasakhah keertirscha maninaa saha
Praadurbhootosmi raashtreasminkeertimriddhi dadaatu mey.

O friend of the gods, bestower of wealth, please bless me with godlike glory, greatness and wealth, fame and prosperity. As I am born in this world, I would like to enjoy all that this world has to offer. May the gods bless me with their glory.

क्षुत्पिपासामलां ज्येष्ठामलक्ष्मीं नाशयाम्यहम्।
अभूतिमसमृद्धिं च सर्वां निर्णुद मे गृहात्।।

*Kshutpipaasaamalaam jyeshthhaamalakshmeem
 naashayaamyaham
Abhootimasamriddhim cha sarvaam nirnud mey
 grihaat.*

As the tree sucks nourishment from the earth, so do all living beings need nourishment from birth to death. They become full of impurities and are perishable. I renounce the energy of Alakshmi that causes poverty and deprivation. O great goddess, destroy all that is transient and bestow upon me intransient opulence by eradicating my sorrows and sins. Bless my abode with opulence and riches.

गन्धद्वारां दुराधर्षां नित्यपुष्टां करीषिणीम्।
ईश्वरीं सर्वभूतानां तामिहोप ह्वये श्रियम्।।

Gandhadvaaraam duraadharshaam nityapushtaam kareeshineem
Eeshvareem sarvabhootaanaam taamihopa hvayey shriyam.

I invoke you, goddess, who delights in being offered fragrant flowers, who is invincible and forever nurturing. Goddess who is the controller of all beings and elements, wealth, grain and prosperity, Mother of all creation, I invoke you.

मनस: काममाकूतिं वाच: सत्यमशीमहि।
पशूनां रूपमन्नस्य मयि श्री: श्रयतां यश:।।

Manasah kaamamaakootim vaachah satyamsheemahi
Pashoonaam roopamannasya mayi shreeh
   shrayataam yashah.

With your grace let my desires be noble and my utterings, truthful. Beloved of Vishnu, the Preserver of the world, with your blessings may I be granted the best food, milk, honour, fame and prosperity.

कर्दमेन प्रजा भूता मयि संभव कर्दम।
श्रियं वासय में कुले मातरं पद्मालिनीम्।।

Kardamena prajaa bhootaa mayi sambhava kardama
Shriyam vaasaya mein kuley maataram
   padmaalineem.

I pray to the rishi Kardama: On my behalf request your mother Lakshmi (Shree) who is the best Mother, the Mother of the universe, who dwells in the lotus, to dwell in my house.*

---

* *Lakshmi's blessings are symbolized by her four mind-born sons: Ananda, or eternal bliss; Kardam or the Kadamba tree, symbolic of the highest of refined energies; Chikleet or fertile land and Shreeya or prosperity.*
Shriyam vaasayam: wherever there is truth, there is love, wherever there is love there is goodwill.

आप सृजन्तु स्निग्धानि चिक्लीत वस मे गृहे।
नि च देवीं मातरं श्रियं वासय मे कुले।।

Aaap srijantu snigdhaani chikleet vasa mey grihey
Ni cha deveen maataram shriyam vaasaya mey kuley.

O Lord Varun, your energy empowers the earth which is blessed with fecundity by the divine nurturing energy of Lakshmi.* May that goddess with her compassion and her nurturing energy, who is blessed with divine attributes and who sustains creation, please dwell in my house forever.

According to the Garuda Purana *the Sun God has twelve different names which correspond with the twelve months of the year. Varun is the name given for the monsoon season, as Lord Varun is supposed to preside over the fertility and abundance of the crops during this season.*

आदीं पुष्करिणीं पुष्टिं पिङ्गलां पद्ममालिनीम्।
चन्द्रां हिरण्मयीं लक्ष्मीं जातवेदो म आ वह।।

*Aadraam pushkarineem pushtim pingalaam
    padmamaalineem
Chandraam hiranmayeem Lakshmeem jaatavedo
    ma aa vaha.*

May the goddess through her compassion send abundant rain and nourish creation. May reservoirs of water grace the earth like a garland of lotuses. O god of fire, please invoke Lakshmi of the soothing countenance, like that of the moon, to reside in my place of dwelling.

आर्द्रां य: करिणीं यष्टि सुवर्णा हेममालिनीम्।
सूर्यां हिरण्मयीं लक्ष्मीं जातवेदो म आ वह।।

*Aardraam yah karineem yashti suvarnaa
   hemamaalineem
Suryaam hiranmayeem Lakshmeem jaatavedo ma
   aa vaha.*

O god of fire, please help me invoke that great goddess Lakshmi who blesses those dear to her and punishes the evil; who adorns herself with a golden garland and is beauty personified; who nourishes creation with knowledge, prosperity and opulence as the sun nourishes the earth with rain and light.

तां म आ वह जातवेदो लक्ष्मीमनपगामिनीम्।
यस्यां हिरण्यं प्रभूतं गावो दास्योऽश्वानविन्देयं पुरुषानहम्।।

Taam ma aa vaha jaatavedo
 Lakshmeemanapagaamineem
Yasyaam hiranyam prabhootam gaavo
 daasyoshvaanvindeyam purushaanaham.

O god of fire, for my good, please help me invoke the goddess who can bless me so that I may pray to her to fulfil my desire for enjoying the best of health, prosperity, many servants and good horses, sons and grandsons.

य: शुचि: प्रयतो भूत्वा जुहुयादाज्यमन्वहम्।
सूक्तं पंचदशर्चं च श्रीकाम: सततं जपेत्।।

*Yah shuchih prayato bhootvaa
    juhuyaadaajyamanvaham
Sooktam panchadasharcha cha shreekaamah
    satatam japet.*

He who is desirous of receiving the blessings of Lakshmi should, after purifying his mind and body and disciplining his senses, offer clarified butter to the fire daily while chanting these fifteen verses of the Shree Sooktam.

THE LAKSHMI SOOKTA

The Lakshmi Sookta is a hymn which belongs to the post-Vedic period when people had begun practising direct invocation, without offering their prayers through Agni, the god of fire. God became a more personalized entity so a direct dialogue took place between the devotee and the personal deity. Post-Vedic prayers, therefore, make no mention of the havan or fire sacrifice.

The Lakshmi Sookta is a prayer addressed directly to the goddess of abundance and good fortune.

पद्मानने पद्मिनि पद्मपत्रे पद्मप्रिये पद्मदलायताक्षि।
विश्वप्रिये विश्वमनोऽनुकूले त्वत्पादपद्मं मयि सन्निधत्स्व।।

Padmaananey padimani padmapatrey
　padmapriyey padmadalaayataakshi
Vishvapriyey vishvamanonukooley
　tvatpaadapadmam mayi sannidhatsva.

O lotus-faced Lakshmi, who is seated on a lotus and wears a garland of lotuses, your lotus-like eyes are full of compassion. Every worldly being prays to you for his or her well-being. I pray to you O great goddess who always fulfils desire. May your divine lotus feet dwell in my heart.

पद्मानने पद्मउरू पद्माक्षी पदमसंभवे।
तन्मे भजसि पद्माक्षि येन सौख्यं लभाम्यहम्।।

*Padmaananey padmauroo padmaakshee
    padmasambhavey
Tanmey bhajasi padmaakshi yena saukhyam
    labhaamyaham.*

O you whose eyes, face and form resemble the lotus, and who is born of a lotus, I pray to you to bless me with your compassionate grace. Please always look upon me with benign favour.

अश्वदायि गोदायि धनदायि महाधने।
धनं मे जुषतां देवि सर्वकामाश्च देहि मे।।

Ashvadaayi godaayi dhanadayi mahaadhaney
Dhanam mey jushataam devi sarvakaamaashcha
   dehi mey.

O great goddess Lakshmi, you are capable of bestowing riches and worldly comforts like transport and nourishment. Kindly bless me with all these and fulfil all my worldly desires.

पुत्रं पौत्रं धनं धान्यं हस्त्यश्वादि गवेरथम्।
प्रजानां भवसि माता आयुष्मन्तं करोतु मे।।

*Putram pautram dhanam dhaanyam
    hastyashvaadi gaveratham
Prajaanaam bhavasi maataa aayushmantam
    karotu mey.*

O great goddess, you are the Mother of all creation. Please bless me with good progeny, riches and opulence of every kind and longevity to enjoy it all.

धनमग्निधनं वायुर्धनं सूर्यो धनं वसुः।
धनमिन्द्रो वृहस्पतिर्वरुणो धनमस्तु मे।।

*Dhanamagnidhanam vayurdhanam sooryo
    dhanam vasuh
Dhanamindro vrihaspatirvaruno dhanamastu
    mey.*

O Mother Lakshmi, please bless me with the purest of the five elements of air, earth, water, fire and ether which nourish my body. Bless me to receive this grace and bounty through Vishnu the Preserver and the benevolent Varuna, the nurturing element of the Sun God.

वैनतेय सोमं पिब सोमं पिबतु वृत्रहा।
सोमं धनस्य सोमिनो मह्यं ददातु सोमिनः।।

Vainateya somam piba somam pibatu vritrahaa
Somam dhanasya somino mahyam dadaatu
   sominah.

Lord Indra, the annihilator of the possessive instinct, borne in a pot by Garuda, the son of Vinta, bless me with the wealth of immortality.*

---

* *Lord Vishnu, seated on Garuda, carried the pot of the nectar of immortality.*

न क्रोधो न च मात्सर्यं न लोभो नाशुभामतिः।
भवन्ति कृतपुण्यानां भक्तानां श्री सूक्तजापिनाम्।।

*Na krodho na cha maatsarya na lobho
    naashubhaamatih
Bhavanti kritapunyaanaam bhaktaanaam shree
    sooktajaapinaam.*

The one who prays to you daily with devotion shall cease to indulge in lower emotions such as jealousy, anger, greed and evil actions.

सरसिजनिलये सरोजहस्ते धवलतरांशुक गन्धमाल्यशोभे।
भगवति हरिवल्लभे मनोज्ञे त्रिभुवनभूतिकरि प्रसीद मह्याम्।।

*Sarasijanilayey sarojahastey dhavalataraanshuka
   gandhamaalyashobhey
Bhagavati harivallabhey manogyey
   tribhuvanabhootikari praseeda mahyam.*

O great goddess, who dwells in a pond full of lotuses, who bears lotus flowers on her body and in her hands, who wears clean, brilliant white clothes and a fragrant sandalwood garland; the beloved of Vishnu who can reach the minds of beings in all the three worlds—the physical, astral and causal—Tribhuvaneshwari, I seek your blessings in all humility.

विष्णुपत्नीं क्षमां देवीं माधवीं माधवप्रियाम्।
लक्ष्मीं प्रियसखीं देवीं नमाम्यच्युतवल्लभाम्।।

*Vishnupatneem kshamaam deveem maadhaveem
    maadhavapriyaam
Lakshmeem priyasakheem deveem
    namaamyachyutavallabhaam.*

O beloved wife of Lord Vishnu the Preserver, who is the epitome of compassion, and is imbued with the sweetness of honey, beloved companion of Vishnu, I pay obeisance to you repeatedly.

महालक्ष्म्यै च विद्महे विष्णुपत्न्यै।
च धीमही तन्नो लक्ष्मी: प्रचोदयात्।।

*Mahaalakshmyaiy cha vidmahey vishnupatnyaiy
Cha dheemahee tanno Lakshmeeh prachodayaat.**

---

* *This shloka alone can be chanted as a mantra.*

O great goddess I invoke you. I meditate upon you. Please bless me always and encourage me towards doing good.

चंद्रप्रभां लक्ष्मीमेशानीं सूर्याभांलक्ष्मीमेश्वरीम्।
चंद्र सूर्याग्निसंकाशां श्रियं देवीमुपास्महे।।

*Chandraprabhaam Lakshmeemeshaaneem
 suryaambhaalakshmeemeshvareem
Chandra suryaagnisankaashaam shriyam
 deveemupaasmahey.*

I pray to that Lakshmi, who, as the sun and the moon radiate in the sky, radiates both the glow of the moon and the brilliant light of the sun.

श्री वर्चस्वमायुष्यमारोग्यमाविधाच्छोभमानं महीयते।
धान्यं धनं पशु बहुतपुत्रलाभं शतसंवत्सरं दीर्घमायुः।।

Shree varchasvamaayushyamaarogyamaavidhaa-
   chhobhamaanam maheeyatey
Dhaanyam dhanam pashu bahutaputralaabham
   shatsamvatsaram deerghamaayuh.

The one who recites the Lakshmi Sookta is blessed with riches, glory, a long life, good health, children and sustenance. Such a man himself is praised by others for thousands of years.

Kshamaa Praarthanaa
A Prayer Seeking Forgiveness

O great goddess, nurturer of the world and protector of beings, please forgive any inadequacy in my worship of you and any omissions I may have unknowingly committed. For as your child, you know I am not perfect but I do seek your blessings for the attainment of perfection.

Appendix

Mantras for the goddess Lakshmi

ॐ ऐं श्रीं ह्रीं क्लीं।
Aum Aeng Shreem Hreem Kleem

ॐ श्रीं महालक्ष्म्यै नमः।
Aum Shreem Mahalakshmyey Namah

ॐ श्रीं ह्रीं महालक्ष्म्यै नमः।
Aum Shreem Hreem Mahalakshmyey Namah

महादैव्यै च विद्धटमहे विष्णुपत्न्यै
च धीमही तन्नो लक्ष्मी: प्रचोदयात्।।
*Mahaadaivyaiy cha viddhatamahey Vishnupatnyaiy
Cha dheemahee tanno Lakshmeeh prachodayaat.*

About the Author

Ashima Singh is a pranic healer-teacher and former media person based in New Delhi who has conducted self-awareness and personal growth workshops in many countries. She has studied the religious philosophy, art and literature of many cultures in her quest to relate to the energy force that binds all humanity. She imparts to this book her keen awareness and knowledge of this energy force and talks about how it can have a positive effect on our lives.